Emotional Stability
Beating Bipolar Disorder

BY

Pastor Rick Carter Jr. Ph.D.

Emotional Stability

ISBN: 978-1-60208-444-5

Table of Contents

THE SOURCE OF THE PROBLEM

Over the last number of years, I hear more and more people identify themselves as bipolar. Many have been diagnosed with this disorder by psychiatrists and as a result carry the label around their neck as a chain describing their up-and-down emotional condition. Bipolar disorder used to be called manic depressive, but it was relabeled a few years ago. Today, nearly anyone who feels up sometimes and down at other times is labeled as bipolar. In some ways, this is just part of the human condition; there is a natural up and down emotional cycle inherent in the body. In other ways, emotional highs and lows can be exaggerated in some people for various reasons.

Certainly there can be physiological issues that are brought on by any number of means. Illness, injury, childbirth, reproductive organ or glandular failure are just a few issues that can create a genuine chemical imbalance in an individual, and in such cases, these things should be treated in an appropriate way. There are tests can be given that will determine the level of certain chemicals in the blood, brain and nervous system; often a test for the level of certain hormones the body produces is only given when there is physical issue manifested such as muscle pain, joint pain, issues with muscle coordination or the like. These actual physiological issues are not what I intend to address, and I will leave the actual physical medial issues to the medical doctors. What does concern me is that when a person is having emotional issues, it is common for doctors to prescribe medication to change their behavior rather than trying resolve a physical issue or even check to see if there is a "chemical imbalance". I have counseled with some who were given medication simply by telling their doctors they were feeling down or anxious without ever having any chemical tests at all; simply throwing drugs at a problem does not solve the problem. I have been told by some that while the drugs did take away their negative feelings, it actually left them with no feelings at all. Far from creating happiness or peace, the medications left them completely empty and dead feeling inside. Some of these chemical treatments can even create more harm than good, as each has possible side effects that can be very severe, including actual physical damage that can lead to death. While doctors can measure the amount of certain chemicals and hormones in the body, there is no chemical test that can be run to actually identify depression or anxiety, though we know that there are certain chemicals released during these times that contribute to those feelings; why our bodies release these chemicals is the bigger question. Is it a truly physiological issue such as a damaged organ or gland, or is it more of a reaction to other stimuli?

I am certain that the answer you get will depend on who you are asking and what vested interest they have. A doctor who must answer to a board or hospital must work according to the requirements of their employer and within the confines of health insurance requirements in order to receive payment for their services. Often there is pressure for doctors to come to a quick diagnosis and launch a treatment quickly that will produce observable results. However, is that in the best interest of the individual? Is it possible that the issues we face have a deeper relationship to our spiritual condition than just our chemical balance? I submit that this is exactly the truth. I am not saying that someone cannot have a genuine physiological problem because of an actual physical sickness, or because of the removal of an organ or gland for some legitimate reason, the chemicals must now be replaced in an artificial manner. I am saying that these cases are rare, and the use of chemicals to treat people whose bodies otherwise function properly is not the best way to deal with feelings. It is more akin to manipulation than it is medicine.

Spiritually we see a pattern in the Bible in the book of James that will help us to identify the issue of the up and down feelings that many experience. Look with me in the first chapter and let's read verses 2-8.

"My brethren, count it all joy when ye fall into divers temptations; Knowing this, that the trying of your faith worketh patience. But let patience have her perfect work, that ye may be perfect and entire, wanting nothing. If any of you lack wisdom, let him ask of God, that giveth to all men liberally, and upbraideth not; and it shall be given him. But let him ask in faith, nothing wavering. For he that wavereth is like a wave of the sea driven with the wind and tossed. For let not that man think that he shall receive any thing of the Lord. A double minded man is unstable in all his ways."

Notice a few things about this description. The wavering or double minded person goes up and down without control. They are tossed, the Bible says here, and have no ability to achieve stability on their own. If you have ever been in a boat during a storm, you will understand the picture that is used here. You are subject to the movement of the waves, your boat moves up and down with the movement of the water. This is an interesting description that seems to correspond well with the description of someone who is called bipolar: they are tossed up and down emotionally without the ability to control their emotional condition. It isn't that they don't want to have control, it just seems to be beyond their grasp. In a boat, someone may experience sea sickness, a physical condition that is the result of the continual upheaval. You can even take medication to deal with that issue, however the true cure is to get out of the rough water and back to smooth seas. In a sense, this is what happens when a person is taken out of their environment and placed in a secluded one such as a hospital. The turmoil that

7

had you sick is removed and the removal of the stresses of life allow your water to be calmed.

Suffice it to say that the secular approach to treating these ups and downs is to use a combination of medication, hospitalization (for the purpose of isolation), and then counseling therapy. This is not far different than what you might receive if you get sea sick: medication with Dramamine, hospitalization or isolation off of the boat, and then having to be convinced by someone to get back on the boat. Thus, the comparison of bipolar and sea sickness is a very appropriate model.

Let's now turn our attention to what it is that causes our life to be driven in such a way as to create the ups and downs that we have discussed. In the text that we

**Temptation:
The enticement to
forsake your faith**

referenced in James, we see two driving factors: temptations and trials. These each work in a slightly different fashion.

Temptations are an attempt to draw you away from your faith by enticing your lusts. The lusts of the flesh are unrelenting,

Temptation:
Causes us to reach upward emotionally for the promise of the fulfilment of our lusts.

and even those things that we know are to be avoided are ever before us. When Jesus was tempted on the mountain, He faced the same three types of

8

temptation that John warns us about in 1 John 2:16 "For all that is in the world, the lust of the flesh, and the lust of the eyes, and the pride of life, is not of the Father, but is of the world." Temptation pulls on our lusts to draw us away from the Father and into the world. It is pictured here as the uprising of the wave not because it elevates us, but rather because it is the rising up of the rule of the flesh in our lives. It is saying that you can rule your own life, you can have your own desires, you can forsake the faith that you have in God, and let your flesh have control. Just as Adam and Eve reached upward toward the fruit of the tree in the garden, they were falling; so it is in our own lives. Temptation never produces the fruit of fulfillment in our lives that it promises, it always leaves us empty inside and destitute of satisfaction. Strangely, though, we continue to chase after its vain promise to the destruction of our souls. If only we had what our soul lusts after, then we would be happy, then we would be content, then we would be... Constantly chasing our lusts is a sure plan for continual turmoil in our lives and it will never provide stability because lusts are never satisfied; there is always something more to attain and we can never have it all.

Trials, on the other hand, are an attempt to cause us to question the validity and certainty of our faith. It is when we begin to question our faith or confidences that we are prone to the turmoil of our circumstances. Solomon writes in Proverbs 14:26, "In the fear of the

Trial:
The affliction of the foundation of your faith.

Trials

LORD is strong confidence: and his children shall have a place of refuge." As trials rage against us, they are beating against the foundation of our faith, trying to tear away at the anchor that holds us through the storm. Satan loves to get us unmoored from our faith, because then we are completely subject to the waves of temptation and trial. This is true not only with regard to our faith in God, but also in relationship to any number of confidences that people may have.

An unbeliever may have set their confidence or faith in their family, their education, their career, their talents, or any number of other things. As long as these things seem stable and strong, they may have little trouble with the drastic drifts of emotion. As soon as their foundation

Trial:
Pushes you downward because they attack against the foundation of your faith.

begins to crumble, however, they will be set adrift. People who seem to be stable for a long period of time and are suddenly struck with the emotional instability characterizes this issue. While one might be tempted to say that a Christian, because their faith is in God, should never have such and experience, they would be forgetting that most people have a good number of confidences that they lean on in life, even as believers. Tell me, if today your spouse died could you declare that you would have no emotional trauma? If so, then your marriage is probably in trouble. It is, of course, the hope that our faith in God is strong and will see us through the trial. It is precisely for that reason that God allows trials: to help us to see the extent of our faith, or to see the exact placement of our faith at times.

THE STABALIZING FACTORS

The fact that temptations and trials work in opposite ways is exemplified in James 1:9-11.

"Let the brother of low degree rejoice in that he is exalted: But the rich, in that he is made low: because as the flower of the grass he shall pass away. For the sun is no sooner risen with a burning heat, but it withereth the grass, and the flower thereof falleth, and the grace of the fashion of it perisheth: so also shall the rich man fade away in his ways."

Notice that in both instances there is movement. In the first, from that which is low to an exalted position, and in the second, from that which is high to a depressed position. Temptation is the upswing and trials are the down. Everyone is equal in the fact that they will either be tempted or tried depending upon where they are in life or in different areas of life. A person who is poor will be tempted by possessions and exalted position and even pride in their person as though they had made something of themselves. Yet in other ways, when a person feels they are on top of the world the trials that wear against us will try to bring us down. The question is, how do you endure the ups and downs of life which we will all face? How do you endure the temptations that seek to exalt you and the trials which seek to depress you?

The Bible is very clear here: the stabilizing factors in this process are faith and patience. Faith can be described as simply being confident or certain that something is true or that it works. The purpose of temptations and trials are to help us determine where our faith is genuine and where it is fake. Genuine faith produces patience when faced with temptations and trials; fake faith, however, produces hypocrisy that is revealed when confronted with the same issues. Throughout the book of James, this issue is presented

11

in a variety of ways. The pattern that becomes clear is that if you begin with genuine faith, it will produce a noticeable function or work, which in turn will produce the feelings or affections that accompany our faith.

It is important to understand this pattern: assurance produces actions which produce affections, or faith produces function which produces feelings. This is the proper view of life as seen in James. However, if we confuse faith with feelings, as so often is the case, if we are looking for a feeling instead of basing our beliefs upon a certain confidence, then we will not achieve the same results. Because feelings that produce functions will produce frustration. If our actions are based upon our feelings or the pursuit of feelings, then we will not have the same results. The result of this will instead be hypocrisy, which is spoken of extensively in James.

Notice the contrast of genuine faith and hypocritical faith beginning in James 1:22

> Hearing vs. doing – 1:22-25
>
> Genuine religion vs. Vain religion – 1:26-27
>
> Respect of God vs. respect of men – 2:1-10
>
> Personal obedience vs. judging others – 2:11-13
>
> Compassion vs. neglect – 2:14-16

This is why James teaches that it isn't what we say but what we do that reveals the true nature of our faith. As we said earlier, genuine faith produces works that are evident in their nature. However, a fake faith, one that is in word only when faced with temptation and trials, will be evidenced by the error that it produces and it will crumble when confronted. James spells it out in this fashion in chapter 2 verses 17-26.

"Even so faith, if it hath not works, is dead, being alone. Yea, a man may say, Thou hast faith, and I have works: shew me thy faith without thy works, and I will shew thee my faith by my works. Thou believest that there is one God; thou doest well: the devils also believe, and tremble. But wilt thou know, O vain man, that faith without works is dead? Was not Abraham our father justified by works, when he had offered Isaac his son upon the altar? Seest thou how faith wrought with his works, and by works was faith made perfect? And the scripture was fulfilled which saith, Abraham believed God, and it was imputed unto him for righteousness: and he was called the Friend of God. Ye see then how that by works a man is justified, and not by faith only. Likewise also was not Rahab the harlot justified by works, when she had received the messengers, and had sent them out another way? For as the body without the spirit is dead, so faith without works is dead also."

Since genuine faith is the force that produces stability in our lives, what is it that this faith must be based on? For the person who is not trusting in God, they may base their confidence or faith in their abilities, their loved ones, their career, or some other life factor that they have chosen. When their confidence in this factor is shaken, then their stabilizing force is removed, and they become tossed with the waves of temptation and trial. Ultimately, they are looking for another stabilizing force to grab onto.

This, of course, is not what God wants because everything that you will find in this world is temporary. Our abilities diminish, our loved ones die, our careers end, economies crash, society changes; there is nothing certain in this world at all. That doesn't mean that there is nothing that can bring stability to our emotional state, however, because despite the uncertainty of this world, there is someone who transcends this world and never changes. That truth is revealed in James 1:17-18.

"Every good gift and every perfect gift is from above, and cometh down from the Father of lights, with whom is no variableness, neither shadow of turning. Of his own will begat he us with the word of truth, that we should be a kind of firstfruits of his creatures."

God isn't driven by the issues of this world; He is constant, He never changes. We are reminded of this truth in the last book of the Old Testament. It says in Malachi 3:6, "For I am the LORD, I change not; therefore ye sons of Jacob are not consumed." There is no changing in God, He is the same yesterday, today and forever according to Hebrews 13:8. As James says, there is no variableness or shadow of turning. That means that He is stable and consistent at all times, and as such, you can cling to Him when the issues of life are trying to toss you up and down. Not only is God Himself our source of confidence, but according to the verses in James we last saw, the word of truth is stable and used by God. That means that we can trust the Bible and have confidence that it is true. The Word of God also does not change, it is forever settled in heaven (Psalm 119:89), and we can hold it in our hands.

I believe that the two types of gifts spoken of here are the results of enduring temptation and trial. A good gift is the result of overcoming temptation. Through facing temptation, we learn what is good and what is evil. We are tempted to do evil, and thus, are able to identify more distinctly what is good. By learning this, we grow in the fear of the LORD. Often when we are first saved, we don't readily understand what is good and what is evil. There are some things that we do of which we are ignorant concerning their evil nature. When we learn the truth, however, we are then faced with the temptation to continue in those things. In this fashion, the good gift is God's way of revealing the path to growing in Christ's likeness. When we choose the fear of the LORD, we depart from evil and temptation and choose to embrace the good that God has shown us.

The perfect gift is the opportunity to face a trial, that may sound like a far-fetched idea but follow my thinking here for a moment. We have already been told in James 1:3-4, "Knowing this, that the trying of your faith worketh patience. But let patience have her perfect work, that ye may be perfect and entire, wanting nothing." Here we learn that we are perfected by learning patience and we learn patience by trials, so we can then draw the conclusion that trials are a perfecting gift or stated differently they are a gift that perfects us. We have been wrongly told to be fearful of trials and try to avoid them or get out of them as soon as you possibly can, but why would we fear what God has clearly told us will make us perfect in Him? I am not being strange here, I realize that trials are hard and uncomfortable but don't you want to be perfect in Christ? Don't you want to bring Him glory? This can only happen to a greater degree when you accept that trials are a way of perfecting your faith, that makes them a gift.

James 3:14-16 "But if ye have bitter envying and strife in your hearts, glory not, and lie not against the truth.   This wisdom descendeth not from above, but is earthly, sensual, devilish.   For where envying and strife is, there is confusion and every evil work."

THE FAULTS EXPOSED

The alternate to trusting in God and His Word is to trust in the world and our own thinking. While we might be able to maintain a façade of faith for a while when the temptations and trials of life come the truth will be revealed. One of the first evidences to whether our faith is genuine is our speech. For this reason, James spends so much time dealing with our words in chapter three. When we are talking out of both sides of our mouth, both good and bad, it is an indication that there is instability under the surface. You can try to hide it all you want, but what is in the heart will come out of the mouth; you cannot hide it forever. Your mouth reveals the iniquity of the heart.

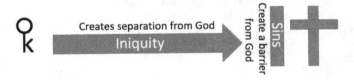

"But your iniquities have separated between you and your God, and your sins have hid *his* face from you, that he will not hear." Isaiah 59:2

Iniquity is not just sin in a general sense, it is really the attitude of your heart either positively toward wickedness or negatively toward righteousness. It is how you really feel on the inside about these things. Isaiah 59:2 says, "But your iniquities have separated between you and your God, and your sins have hid his face from you, that he will not hear." Notice that separation here is created by iniquity and then the sinful transgression that results is what hides God's face from us. So often we deal with the transgression in confession, but we retain the sinful attitude that lead to it at the same time. I remember wondering for years why it was that I fell into the same sins over and over, and you may have the same question. The answer is quite simple. The reason that you fall into that sin is that you have created the right atmosphere for it to appear. The iniquity of your heart is what makes you vulnerable to the transgression. Dealing with the action alone is never going to remove the problem for long. An infection may manifest itself in many different ways, but if all you do is treat the symptoms, then you will become more ill. You must attack the source of the infection if you are to regain health. So often we deal with the symptomatic actions and fail to address the underlying iniquity, which is why we cannot remove the sin permanently.

You can put on the outward appearance of righteousness, but the iniquity of your heart will eventually show through and most often will do so in your words. It says in James 3:6, "And the tongue is a fire, a world of iniquity: so is the tongue among our members, that it defileth the whole body, and setteth on fire the course of nature; and it is set on fire of hell."

There are two distinct issues that are revealed in the tongue that are hidden in the heart according to James 3:14-16.

"But if ye have bitter envying and strife in your hearts, glory not, and lie not against the truth. This wisdom descendeth not from above, but is earthly, sensual, devilish. For where envying and strife is, there is confusion and every evil work."

The first issue that is revealed by the tongue is envy. Envy is not simply jealousy. From a Bible prospective, jealousy is the desire to protect what rightfully belongs to you, whereas envy is the desire to possess or destroy what rightfully belongs to another. Envy sees others who have, and rather than being motivated to earn it for themselves, causes them to simply want others diminished in what they have. Envy, when revealed in your heart, is an indication that you have removed your faith from being in God to being in possessions or position. The lust for these things has taken first place in your heart, and you believe that if you just had what that other person has, then you would be fulfilled or stable in life. In this fashion, envy is a tell that your faith has been misplaced and can be a central reason for instability in your life. I will address this in much greater detail in the next chapter.

The second issue revealed by the tongue is that of strife. A person can simply be a contentious person filled with strife in their heart and as a result they drive away relationships and destroy institutions. Many homes, churches, and work places are destroyed by someone who simply has a contentious spirit of strife in them. A person with this attitude will not let anything go, they seemingly must be right which often puts them in conflict with others. They argue about everything and feel the desperate need to correct everyone else.

One thing I notice is that we are told in the first verse of chapter three, "be not many masters". This means we should not be trying to teach everyone else. This can be a characteristic of those on an emotional upswing, at those times they can think they know everything and are going to show everyone else how it's done. This is an indication of someone who has also removed their faith from being in God and has set it in themselves. They are filled with the pride of their own person. No one is always right, no one knows everything, but the person who is filled with strife thinks that they might, though they say differently that is exactly what their actions and attitude show. They feel that they have not only the right but the responsibility to correct others when they perceive them to be wrong. This strife ultimately causes them to feel isolated and because others will not confirm their beliefs it sets them up for a big letdown.

These two underlying iniquities are evidence of a misplaced confidence or faith which produces an emotional state that is subject to drastic swings of ups and downs as a person is confronted by temptations and trials. In order to correctly deal with the stormy winds of temptation and trial, you must first deal with these underlying issues. I will acknowledge that many who are in this condition think that their faith is in God, but the presence of these inward iniquities is a clear indication according to the Bible that they have misplaced the genuine faith that they may once have had. Notice that the scripture said that the wisdom of the spirit of envy and strife is not from God, it is the opposite. Envy and strife are said here to be earthly, sensual and devilish. Another way to say that would be that they are of the world, the flesh, and the Devil.

Far too often we excuse away these vile attitudes in a show of false humility or simply the putting on of sanctimonious self-righteousness. In order to deal with these issues, you must confess and forsake the iniquity of envy and strife and adjust your misplaced faith back to the proper foundation of God and His Word. It is then that you can begin to deal with temptation and trials in the right way. In order to get a better understanding of how to remove envy and strife from your life, let's take a more detailed look at each.

DEALING WITH ENVY

Some time back while ministering in Oregon, God smiled on our ministry and blessed us by giving us a beautiful building on two acres of property completely debt free. One day, we had no building and were meeting in a rented hall on Sundays, and the next day, we had a building and never paid anything for it out of our pocket. In addition to the building, God also put over $80,000.00 in our bank account. I was beyond excited about what God had done. To me, this was a great miracle and proof that God was still blessing His people. I wanted everyone to know about what God had done, so I put it on several pastoral email lists that I was on, as well as sending it out in our monthly prayer letter. To my great surprise, I got more negative feedback than positive. A few close friends shared how happy they were for me, but I had complete strangers complain that I had cluttered their inbox with my email, an odd response, since they signed up for the email group. I even had one pastor email to tell me that he didn't think that we deserved the building because we hadn't been there long enough. Others started calling to let me know that they could use the money God had provided.

I was shocked at the response, shocked and disheartened. How could everyone not be filled with joy at the great working of God? Why would people get angry that God had blessed us so greatly? The answer to these questions is ENVY. The Webster's 1828 dictionary provides this definition of envy: "Pain, uneasiness, mortification or discontent excited by the sight of another's superiority or success, accompanied with some degree of hatred or malignity, and often or usually with a desire or an effort to depreciate the person, and with pleasure in seeing him depressed. Envy springs from pride, ambition or love, mortified that another has obtained what one has a strong desire to possess."

Generally, when we think of envy, we associate it with jealousy, and we probably use them interchangeably most of the time in our common speech. However, in the Bible, jealousy is never used in a sinful context. In the Bible, jealousy is most often associated as an emotion expressed by God. God is jealous over His people, He is jealous over their worship, and many other things that rightfully belong to Him. The word jealousy also is used in reference to how a man feels when his wife is unfaithful to him, but this is also used in a legitimate and non-sinful manner. As a matter of fact, if you were to give jealousy a Biblical use definition, it would be something like this: "Jealousy is the zealous desire to protect what is rightfully yours."

Envy, on the other hand, is never used in a positive sense. Envy is nearly the exact opposite of jealousy. A working definition of envy could be stated as: "Envy is the zealous desire to possess or destroy what rightfully belongs to someone else." Consider the following direct statements about the sources of envy.

The prosperity of others can produce envy. "For I was envious at the foolish, when I saw the prosperity of the wicked." Psalm 73:3 "For he had possession of flocks, and possession of herds, and great store of servants: and the Philistines envied him." Genesis 26:14

A blessing in the life of another, which you desired yourself, can produce envy. "And when Rachel saw that she bare Jacob no children, Rachel envied her sister; and said unto Jacob, Give me children, or else I die." Genesis 30:1

Simply seeing others earn what they have suffered and worked for can produce envy. "Again, I considered all travail, and every right work, that for this a man is envied of his neighbour. This is also vanity and vexation of spirit." Ecclesiastes 4:4

The desire for personal glory that others have received can produce envy. "Let us not be desirous of vain glory, provoking one another, envying one another." Galatians 5:26

We have all found ourselves in these types of temptations to allow envy to take hold of our hearts. As a matter of fact, the Bible warns us in James 4:5that we are all susceptible to the sin of envy. "Do ye think that the scripture saith in vain, The spirit that dwelleth in us lusteth to envy?" Don't kid yourself; there is no one who is above falling into this sin. The sad reality is that many believers are ensnared with this wickedness and either don't realize it or won't admit it. Envy is one of the worst sinful emotions that you can have! Solomon spoke of the consequences of envy when he said, "A sound heart is the life of the flesh: but envy the rottenness of the bones." Proverbs 14:30. Envy rots you from the inside out. We are warned that it is even worse than being a continual angry person in Proverbs 27:4 "Wrath is cruel, and anger is outrageous; but who is able to stand before envy?"

Consider some of the companion sins that are listed alongside envy in these scriptures.

Romans 1:29 "Being filled with all unrighteousness, fornication, wickedness, covetousness, maliciousness; full of envy, murder, debate, deceit, malignity; whisperers,"

Romans 13:13 "Let us walk honestly, as in the day; not in rioting and drunkenness, not in chambering and wantonness, not in strife and envying."

1 Corinthians 3:3 "For ye are yet carnal: for whereas there is among you envying, and strife, and divisions, are ye not carnal, and walk as men?"

2 Corinthians 12:20 "For I fear, lest, when I come, I shall not find you such as I would, and that I shall be found unto you such as ye would not: lest there be debates, envyings, wraths, strifes, backbitings, whisperings, swellings, tumults:"

Galatians 5:21 "Envyings, murders, drunkenness, revellings, and such like: of the which I tell you before, as I have also told you in time past, that they which do such things shall not inherit the kingdom of God."

1 Timothy 6:4 "He is proud, knowing nothing, but doting about questions and strifes of words, whereof cometh envy, strife, railings, evil surmisings,"

Titus 3:3 "For we ourselves also were sometimes foolish, disobedient, deceived, serving divers lusts and pleasures, living in malice and envy, hateful, and hating one another."

James 3:14 "But if ye have bitter envying and strife in your hearts, glory not, and lie not against the truth."

James 3:16 "For where envying and strife is, there is confusion and every evil work."

1 Peter 2:1 "Wherefore laying aside all malice, and all guile, and hypocrisies, and envies, and all evil speakings,"

It is no surprise that envy is consistently listed as a companion of strife, because envy seeks to destroy those on whom it is focused. As the Vine's expository dictionary says, "envy another of what he has". This produces the confusion and evil work spoken of in James 3:16, because the victim of envy doesn't understand why the possessor of it is attacking them and why they seem to have such a zeal to hurt them.

Four of the most important men in the Bible were the victims of envious attacks. The reason that Joseph was so hated by his brothers is because of envy, as recorded in Genesis and Acts. Genesis 37:11 "And his brethren envied him; but his father observed the saying." Acts 7:9"And the patriarchs, moved with envy, sold Joseph into Egypt: but God was with him," The result of their envy was that they sold Joseph into slavery and faked his death. His brothers, of course, had to suffer the consequence of watching their father mourn for the next 20 years over the loss of their brother, and I do mean mourn for 20 years! This was a constant reminder of what they had done. Even after 20 years when they are questioned on their intentions of buying grain in Egypt, they are still overcome with the guilt of what they did in their envy.

Moses was a victim of envy according to Psalm 106:16 "They envied Moses also in the camp, and Aaron the saint of the LORD." This is likely a reference to the account of Korah and his companions attacking Moses in Numbers 16. The result of Korah's envy was that he led a rebellion among the priests and nearly had the whole congregation of Israel in revolt against Moses' leadership. Of course, we know that God brought extreme judgment on both the leaders of this rebellion and the followers. God opened the earth and swallowed their whole houses, and then fire came from God and consumed 250 men who followed Korah. God's expression against their rebellion could not be more direct of how He feels about envy. It should also be a warning to every pastor that when envy takes hold of someone in their congregation, it can have unbelievably devastating consequences. It is likely that envy is involved in most church conflicts.

We know that the scripture also tells us that it was envy that lead to the crucifixion of our Lord Jesus Christ. Twice this is spoken of as the source of the Jew's resentment of Him. Matthew 27:18 "For he knew that for envy they had delivered him." Mark 15:10 "For he knew that the chief priests had delivered him for envy." The New Testament differs from the Old in its expression of the consequences of envy upon those who gave themselves to it. There are no direct consequences listed in the Bible for those who delivered Christ to be crucified, though there were certainly consequences to the nation of Israel that I believe are direct results of this sinful envy.

The final individual spoken of as directly affected by envy in the Bible record is the apostle Paul. Acts 13:45 says, "But when the Jews saw the multitudes, they were filled with envy, and spake against those things which were spoken by Paul, contradicting and blaspheming." Again, in Acts 17:5, it says, "But the Jews which believed not, moved with envy, took unto them certain lewd fellows of the baser sort, and gathered a company, and set all the city on an uproar, and assaulted the house of Jason, and sought to bring them out to the people." The reality here is that these people may have seemed to escape earthly consequences because of their anger, and their purposes would seem to have been accomplished, but they damned themselves to hell. What could be a greater consequence than that?

While the word envy is not used in connection with any believers in the New Testament, we do see the concept expressed in 3 John 1:9 "I wrote unto the church: but Diotrephes, who loveth to have the preeminence among them, receiveth us not." Obviously, Diotrephes desired the preeminence that the apostles had and caused strife over his

26

desire to possess it. The strife that accompanies envy is devastation to everyone that it touches.

I never like to present a problem without also sharing the fact that the Bible gives us an answer, as well. There are two sides to this answer. First, if you are infected with the sin of envy, you must repent of it and instill two very important factors in your life. Proverbs 23:17 says, "Let not thine heart envy sinners: but be thou in the fear of the LORD all the day long." I believe that the fear of the Lord is a change factor in Proverbs. The fear of the Lord is defined by Proverbs 8:13 as hating evil. It could be said that the fear of the Lord is to see sin from God's perspective and hate it. If you hate envy the way that God hates it, you will not allow it to remain in your heart. The first step is to understand what envy is and does, then you can examine your heart and make sure that it is identified and eliminated.

The second thing that a person must do to prevent envy from returning is alluded to in 1 Corinthians 13:4. "Charity suffereth long, and is kind; charity envieth not; charity vaunteth not itself, is not puffed up," If you have envy toward someone, it is a sure indication that you do not love them like you should. If you loved them properly, your love would prevent envy from encroaching on your heart. If you sense a spirit of envy in your heart, then you must acknowledge that it is sin, view it from God's prospective, and seek God to develop a sincere love for the one which you have felt envy toward.

Let me now examine how you should respond when someone attacks you in envy. In all four examples that we saw in the Bible, I see two prominent expressions by each of the men. First, all four of them express sincere humility in the face of the envious attacks. Neither Joseph, Moses, Jesus, nor Paul rose up and retaliated against their attackers. As a matter of

27

fact, they all humbly went to God in their affliction and sought His assistance. Envy is an overwhelming zeal that consumes the heart of those affected. When we respond to them with an equal zeal, it only bolsters their resolve. They use our zeal against us and draw us into the mud. I have seen people in envy attack someone and that person defends himself or herself. The envious person then says, "See how they are defending themselves? It is obvious that they are trying to hide something because of how they are acting." Trust me when I say that you cannot win the fight against envy by responding in the flesh. Take the admonition of Ephesians 6:12 that "we wrestle not against flesh and blood". Your enemy, when you are attacked by envy, is not the individual; it is the spiritual wickedness that is motivating them. As a believer, we must always remember that we must fight wickedness by spiritual means.

Paul's attitude about those who envied his ministry was uniquely expressed in Philippians 1:15, when he says, "Some indeed preach Christ even of envy and strife; and some also of good will:" Paul was able to consider the attacks that others were making against him as still being able to be used of God. I believe in the overcoming power of the truth. I believe that despite the intentions of others, God can use all things to produce good. That is what Joseph believed when he said to his brothers in Genesis 50:20, "But as for you, ye thought evil against me; but God meant it unto good, to bring to pass, as it is this day, to save much people alive." With this understanding, a humble spirit is the best way to express that you have confidence that God is in control of every situation and that no matter what they intend by their envy, God can and will use it to accomplish what He desires.

Much could be said about the spirit of humility that these men expressed. Suffice it to say that a humble spirit is vital when we are attacked. We are admonished to be like Christ in this specifically in 1 Peter 2:23, when it says, "Who, when he was reviled, reviled not again; when he suffered, he threatened not; but committed himself to him that judgeth righteously:" Humility in this way means that you don't return fire with fire, you do not attack when attacked.

Peter also expresses the second principle that we must express when facing envy here when he says that Jesus "committed himself to him that judgeth righteously". This means that you must not take hold of the situation and decide to deal with it yourself; you must turn it over to God. You must commit your defense to God and earnestly believe that He will judge righteously and be your defense in the storm. I have, unfortunately too often, been quick to defend myself against the attacks of envy, and I have suffered because of it. God has promised over and over to defend His people, and yet we seldom give Him the chance.

If we refuse to respond to the attacks of envy and instead keep a humble spirit and commit the situation to God, we will find that those who are filled with envy will be exposed by their own actions. When they act sinfully and have no response from us to try and justify their vile hatred, others will see the reality of their spirit and know what the source is. Don't get dragged into the devil's traps; keep a humble spirit and trust God to defend you and you will find that envy is defeated.

James 3:14-16 "But if ye have bitter envying and strife in your hearts, glory not, and lie not against the truth. This wisdom descendeth not from above, but is earthly, sensual, devilish. For where envying and strife is, there is confusion and every evil work."

DEALING WITH STRIFE

James 3:13-18 "Who is a wise man and endued with knowledge among you? let him shew out of a good conversation his works with meekness of wisdom. But if ye have bitter envying and strife in your hearts, glory not, and lie not against the truth. This wisdom descendeth not from above, but is earthly, sensual, devilish. For where envying and strife is, there is confusion and every evil work. But the wisdom that is from above is first pure, then peaceable, gentle, and easy to be intreated, full of mercy and good fruits, without partiality, and without hypocrisy. And the fruit of righteousness is sown in peace of them that make peace."

What a contrast we see here between a spirit of strife and the spirit that which God has called us to. The fruit of strife is said here to be confusion and every evil work. Let that sink in a bit. We know according to 1 Corinthians 14:33 that God is not the author of confusion, and we certainly know that He is also not the author of evil works. This reality leaves us with the knowledge that strife is a work of the Evil One. Satan does some of his most prosperous work in the believer when he deceives him into thinking that God would have him to be contentious with others.

The Webster's 1828 Dictionary defines strife as follows: [1]Exertion or contention for superiority; contest of emulation, either by intellectual or physical efforts. [2]Contention in anger or enmity; contest; struggle for victory; quarrel or war.

We might often think of strife from a somewhat positive view such as striving for the faith but many times our strife leaves off a proper place of contending for truth and devolves into simply contention. Some people are in conflict with anyone they come into contact with. Not long ago I told my church that if you have a conflict with everyone you know then it probably isn't them that has the issue. I have known several people who seemed to look for a reason to argue with anyone, and others still who were just contrary towards anything that was said with a positive tone.

We are told in Proverbs 3:30, "Strive not with a man without cause, if he have done thee no harm." The problem is that we are often looking for cause. Might I suggest that someone saying something you disagree with is not itself cause for strife. I know that some won't like that, since we all think that we are on a crusade for truth, however, the reality is that arguments are more often over opinion than over real truth and unless the statement was actually causing harm it doesn't have to be contended for. Paul said in 2 Timothy 2:14 "Of these things put them in remembrance, charging them before the Lord that they strive not about words to no profit, but to the subverting of the hearers."

The reality is that when God describes what the works of the flesh are in Galatians 5, He lists strife right along with adultery, idolatry, witchcraft, and murder. The self-righteous attitude that can be conveyed through a spirit of strife is simply not pleasing to God no matter how right you might think you are. The truth is that pride is at the root of strife itself. Solomon twice addressed this in Proverbs.

Proverbs 28:25 "He that is of a proud heart stirreth up strife: but he that putteth his trust in the LORD shall be made fat."

Proverbs 13:10 "Only by pride cometh contention: but with the well advised is wisdom."

This is the issue brought forward by James with regard to strife, that it reveals the iniquity of pride in the heart, and that this pride results in the forcing of contention with those around us. Such strife naturally brings not only temptation to

32

prove ourselves superior to others, but trials when we drive others away by our contentions. In this fashion, our strife produced by pride provides both elements that create emotional instability. The unique issue, however, much like envy, is sure to be blamed by those who possess it on those around them. Such a person could never admit that they themselves were the source, that it must be that if others would just recognize their superior ideas or arguments and submit to them then the strife would cease. Of course, it would not cease, because the spirit of strife would never die until all had bowed at their feet eternally as if they were on the throne of God themselves. This was, in fact, the great desire of Satan himself.

Solomon told us that once strife had begun it would continue its awful course in Proverbs 17:14 "The beginning of strife is as when one letteth out water: therefore leave off contention, before it be meddled with." Once the water is spilled out it will continue to flow until it reaches equilibrium. In other words, if you spill a glass of water on the table it will flow over the table and down to the chairs and onto the floor. Upon each place, causing trouble and spreading further than you imagined, so it is with strife. It may begin over one issue, but one will spill into another and into another until it has covered the whole house. It is far better not to meddle with it at all than to take the chance of letting it out to begin with.

Paul told us in Philippians 2:3 "Let nothing be done through strife or vainglory". This warning should be sufficient warning to the wise: there is no cause for allowing strife to continue in our hearts. It should be put down with the pride that brings it in at once when it is detected in us. How often it is that we suffer our own vainglory to flourish unchecked, our pride working its wicked way in us until we have eaten sufficiently of its poisoned fruit so that we are right about every thought we have, and others must be told how wrong they are. God help us to rid ourselves of pride and do as Paul continues in the same passage to instruct us, "but in lowliness of mind let each esteem other better than themselves." A good dose of lowliness is in order for all of us so that we would stop looking down on others and consider one another to minister rather than to destroy.

In order to put down strife we must first acknowledge that there is a problem with the iniquity in our own heart and stop blaming others for the strife in our lives. In marriage counseling, I have often reminded people that it takes two people to fight. Once we determine to do away with pride and humble ourselves before God, we can also put away the anger that accompanies pride. If a person is to gain victory over strife, they must also deal with anger in their life. This truth is also addressed by Solomon several times.

Proverbs 15:18 "A wrathful man stirreth up strife: but he that is slow to anger appeaseth strife."

Proverbs 29:22 "An angry man stirreth up strife, and a furious man aboundeth in transgression."

Proverbs 30:33 "Surely the churning of milk bringeth forth butter, and the wringing of the nose bringeth forth blood: so the forcing of wrath bringeth forth strife."

There is a distinct connection here between anger, wrath, and strife. So many blame their anger on those around them, but nothing could be further from the truth. No one can make you angry; you choose to be angry. Anger is not something that comes from the outside; it comes from within the heart. Yielding ourselves to anger does nothing but deceive us into thinking that anger works as a problem-solving technique, which it doesn't. When we yield to anger, we are doing the work of the flesh and such work will never produce the righteousness of God. It is vital that you see that the iniquity of pride which produces strife leads to anger and wrath, once it has been let out it leads us down further sinful paths.

Just as Cain's pride led him to anger and ultimately to hatred and the murder of his brother, the iniquity of pride that is left to run its course leads to the same course in the heart of any man. Proverbs 10:12 says, "Hatred stirreth up strifes". How much further does Solomon need to warn us of the dangers of strife left unchecked in our lives. Surely as James has said it brings about confusion and every evil work.

It saddens me that I have seen strife create divisions in homes and churches. I have seen it infect husbands and wives until it divided the marriage. I have seen strife infect pastors and cause them to tear apart their churches, and likewise, I have seen church members infected by this destructive force and tear apart their church and pastor, as well. It need not be! The reality is that at any moment strife can be ended by a humble spirit and a quieted tongue.

Proverbs 26:20-21 "Where no wood is, there the fire goeth out: so where there is no talebearer, the strife ceaseth. As coals are to burning coals, and wood to fire; so is a contentious man to kindle strife."

If you stop repeating the argument then the strife stops. Of course, that would mean that you have turned away from having to be proven right. What is better than that is that you will have cut off the source of temptation and trials that come as a result of strife. Far too many people in our day have lives filled with strife that will not allow it to end. We might say that they are addicted to the strife or in a more modern phrase, they are addicted to drama; they refuse to let it die. How sad it is that we would perpetuate the drama instead of humbling ourselves to be obedient to God. It may be that you have been feeling tossed by the waves of temptation and trial, and the root of the problem is the strife that you are causing for yourself. I challenge you to take the admonition of Solomon in Proverbs 20:3 "It is an honour for a man to cease from strife: but every fool will be meddling." Don't be a fool, be a person of honor and confess your pride before God, humble yourself and you will find the end of the turmoil that you long for.

DEALING WITH TEMPTATION

Let's talk now about how we are to deal with temptation without allowing it to be a negative driving factor in our lives. Let's begin with understanding the source of temptation. There are two things that we must see in order to have a proper understanding. The first is found in James 1:12-15.

"Blessed is the man that endureth temptation: for when he is tried, he shall receive the crown of life, which the Lord hath promised to them that love him. Let no man say when he is tempted, I am tempted of God: for God cannot be tempted with evil, neither tempteth he any man: But every man is tempted, when he is drawn away of his own lust, and enticed. Then when lust hath conceived, it bringeth forth sin: and sin, when it is finished, bringeth forth death."

First, there is a reward for enduring temptation. The reward is called the crown of life, but I want you to notice what the scripture says about this crown: it is promised to

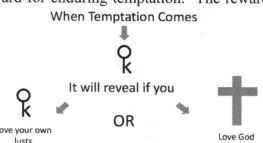

them who love the Lord. Now hold onto that thought. What that means is that your enduring of temptation is a direct evidence of where your love for God is. Now you may not like that as an evaluation but that is what God uses as a barometer here. Temptation reveals if you have a greater love for yourself and your own lusts or a greater love for God.

Second, we must understand that God does not tempt us to do evil, temptation is the result of our own lusts. Every person has a natural bent toward sinful behavior. Lust is a universal problem but each of us responds to it in unique ways based upon what we perceive our needs to be. Perceived needs can run the gambit of issues and it is not our intention here to detail every way in which we could and have allowed ourselves to be tempted by lusts, but rather to simply state an obvious fact: our lusts are uniquely designed within us to seek to fulfill our perceived needs and that these lusts are the source of our temptation to fill our perceived need with sinful behavior rather than righteousness.

So what we see is that temptation brings up a conflict between our lusts and our love for God. The question ultimately comes down to who we love the most ourselves or our Lord.

When our lusts are filled with sinful deeds and we are given to them, the end result is death. This is true both spiritually, emotionally, and physically. A person who gives themselves over to the iniquity of envy or strife and a lack of proper faith kills their relationship with God (not that a person can lose their salvation, but rather that they stop having any fellowship with Him), kills their relationships with others, and ultimately may consider ending their own life because they see no hope of anything changing.

A person cannot have fellowship with God in this state because they are holding onto their iniquity rather than repenting of it. It says in Psalm 66:18, "If I regard iniquity in my heart, the Lord will not hear me:". They cannot have fellowship with others because they are consumed with the desire to take or destroy what others possess, and they cannot have a right mind within themselves because they are consumed with a spirit of failure or despair at their circumstances. though they might not always be able to explain that.

Thus, temptation, which we see as the opportunity for something better than what we have, ultimately brings us down because it is a fantasy, it is fake and does not fulfill what we saw as its promise. The answer is found in chapter 4 of James. He begins in the first four verses by examining the nature of the conflict that we have.

"From whence come wars and fightings among you? come they not hence, even of your lusts that war in your members? Ye lust, and have not: ye kill, and desire to have, and cannot obtain: ye fight and war, yet ye have not, because ye ask not. Ye ask, and receive not, because ye ask amiss, that ye may consume it upon your lusts. Ye adulterers and adulteresses, know ye not that the friendship of the world is enmity with God? whosoever therefore will be a friend of the world is the enemy of God. Do ye think that the scripture saith in vain, The spirit that dwelleth in us lusteth to envy?"

Notice here the three levels of conflict that come because of giving into our lusts. First, we see the internal conflict, war with self: these lusts war in our members, meaning that there is a battle raging inside every one of us concerning our lustful desires. How we respond to that battle is what matters. The natural result of following our lusts is given in verse 5:, that our spirit lusts to envy, the very attitude of iniquity that we saw in chapter 3. Eventually lust will come to a point of envy where we desire to have what rightfully belongs to another. We will even think that we deserve that more than the one who rightfully possesses it currently. This will, of course, lead to the second level of conflict.

This second level of conflict is an external one, war with others. We kill and war with one another, all trying to fulfill our lusts. In the battle to fulfill our lusts, we abuse one another, attack one another, and view everyone else as an obstacle to be overcome so that we can be fulfilled. This conflict means that we see others as a means to our own ends, no longer looking at others who are created in the image of God and as those to whom we can show the love of God, but rather as instruments of our own selfish desires, just tools to satisfy our wants. Whether it is by taking what belongs to them or using them in some other fashion, when we are ruled by our lusts and envy we are at odds with a godly view of others.

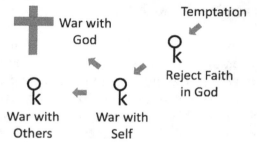

The third area of conflict is the spiritual conflict that inevitably results; this is war with God. We have not because we ask not, which speaks of not coming to God in prayer. When we are seeking to fulfill our own lusts, we don't seek God because we are focused on self and sin. An unfortunate side effect of being filled with the iniquities of envy and strife is that you probably don't even realize that you are not trusting in God. Many people who are in this situation most likely certainly believe that they are trusting in God and are having the problems they face because others are in the wrong. Some will ask God to help them fulfill their lusts thinking that it is doing His will. This is addressed by noting that God is not going to help anyone fulfill sinful lusts even if they ask Him. The area of temptation and the drawing away in our lusts is a major battle ground in our lives.

When we first give into our lusts we are filled with the energy of their promise. We think that this will satisfy my desires or meet my needs. We might go some time in that faith but it is a false confidence. Ultimately what we find is a dead end and that lusts never bring the satisfaction that we thought they would. The letdown for this is real. Depending on how far we went in our temptation pursing the appeasement of our lusts, we can be crushed when we finally hit bottom and realize that it had no real answer. The downer can be greater than the high, and usually is. We call it guilt or regret, and it can easily lead to depression when we see that there is no answer in following our lust and we don't now know where to turn.

Some begin to look for another avenue to try and fulfill that lust which they believe will bring them back up out of the downer, however if that is the path that you choose you will eventually just wind back up in the same place only even harder next time.

The real answer to dealing with temptation is found in James 4:6-10.

"But he giveth more grace. Wherefore he saith, God resisteth the proud, but giveth grace unto the humble. Submit yourselves therefore to God. Resist the devil, and he will flee from you. Draw nigh to God, and he will draw nigh to you. Cleanse your hands, ye sinners; and purify your hearts, ye double minded. Be afflicted, and mourn, and weep: let your laughter be turned to mourning, and your joy to heaviness. Humble yourselves in the sight of the Lord, and he shall lift you up."

This begins with a recognition that it is the grace of God that you need rather than the fulfillment of your lusts. You must forsake your lusts, which are a wrong place to put your confidence, and put your faith back in the God who never changes. Many are too proud to do this, insisting that they just haven't pursued their lusts enough; surely if they pursue them enough, eventually they will meet the promise of satisfaction that they seem to hold. In such a situation, the Bible says that God resists us. In other words, God withholds His grace for overcoming the problems of life from us. His grace for living is withdrawn and we must face the consequences of our sinful decisions alone, often falling further into bitterness, envy and strife.

However, when we humble ourselves by submitting to God's Word, we will experience a far different outcome. The accuser is cast away when we turn to God. When we persist in our lusts, we are subject to the accusation of the Devil against us, but when we confess and forsake our sin, we are covered by the grace of God and there is no more accusation that has power over us.

That is why the Bible tells us here to cleanse our hands and purify our hearts, to cast aside our double-mindedness. That harkens back to the very place we began. When we started this study, we noted that it was a lack of genuine faith that caused us to lack the patience to endure temptations and trials, and made us subject to the ups and downs of life. It was this wavering that was said to be double minded, not set upon a fixed course but fluctuating between what God said and what we thought. We want God's blessings, we just want to get them our own way and we cannot accomplish that.

There is a three-part process presented here that if followed will restore peace with God. First in verse seven, we are to submit to God. Submitting to God is acknowledging that He is right and we are wrong. Some have the wrong idea that they are submitting to God as long as they do a form of what

He has said on those things they like or agree with. Nothing could be further from the truth, it isn't submission when you already agree, submission begins when you don't agree but with a right spirit accept and do what has been asked. Submission to the Divine will is contrary to the natural will but a whole sale acceptance of God's truth is the only path to fully escape the waves of temptation that threaten to overwhelm the soul. Submitting to God means that you stop battling within between God's will and your own, that you come to peace within that He is right and His ways are higher than your own and His thoughts are higher than yours. It means that you finally accept that He alone knows how to make life work and you surrender your own plans to Him.

The second step is to humble yourself to God. In submission, you have abandon your plans for God's now you must lift Him up in your heart and give Him the exalted place that He deserves. For so many, God is placed on equal footing in their view to themselves. You may not think that applies to you, but it most certainly does. You have ignorantly eaten of the tree of the knowledge of good and evil. Like every other person, you weigh the value and benefit of your thoughts against the Word of God as though they held similar or equal weight; they most certainly do not. "Let God be true and every man a liar" Paul says in Romans 3:4. Humility puts God back in His rightful place as Sovereign of your life and truth. True humility might rightly be called complete surrender in the Christian life.

There is a false humility that makes its rounds in Christian circles. This false humility places emphasis on the failure of the flesh. This flesh focused humility is not genuine, it is the attempt of the flesh to appear humble and spiritual. To cause others to think that you have some level of spiritual temperature that is conjured up by your own labors is not humility, it is vain religion. True humility is God focused not man focused. True humility does not say look at how wretched I am, but look at how glorious God is. When others see in in us how exalted God is, they won't need for us to point out how wicked we are, the comparison will be evident in their own lives. This is true humility, God is not exalted by me tearing down self and exposing my past sinful ways. It is by my lifting Him up, talking of His glory and living according to genuine submission that others see how wonderful He is, and in seeing this, humility is impressed upon their souls, as well.

False humility will never end conflict with others, and as a matter of fact, it most certainly increases our battles because we are fussing over who is the most humble at that point. True humility makes all men equal and only God as exalted, and in such a manner, we are at peace with our fellow man, all equally needing the mercy and grace of our God rather than trying to clamor for some level of position to be favored in.

The final and most obvious part of this process is that when we truly submit to God and humble ourselves to Him, we will know what genuine repentance is. True repentance is a gift from 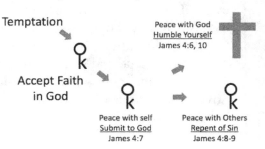 God to the acknowledging of the truth. It comes when we have come to the end of self and see God as the only refuge of hope, which He is.

This is true in salvation as well as our daily life as a believer. Someone who sees an alternative means of refuge is not

44

genuinely saved; they have a Christ of convenience. As soon as a more convenient situation comes along, they will jump from faith in Christ to faith in their new love. This is the scourge of easy believe-ism that has plagued our land; the idea that a person need only recite some magic words without any genuine change of heart is heretical. This is also why believers struggle with conversion from sinful activity in the Christian life: they have a false understanding of repentance. Repentance is what happens when you come to the end of what you have believed completely and recognize that God on His throne must be worshiped and obeyed. You come to Him and He grants you repentance to the acknowledging of the truth. It is that moment when God changes your mind from double to single.

Therefore, true repentance could never be said to be a work of the flesh; it is decidedly a work of the Spirit of God within us that is the response to submission and genuine humility to the Divine will. Some propose a flesh- or mind-based repentance that is the conjuring up of enough of your own will to make a change, but this is certainly not what God proposes.

2 Timothy 2:25-26 "In meekness instructing those that oppose themselves; if God peradventure will give them repentance to the acknowledging of the truth; And that they may recover themselves out of the snare of the devil, who are taken captive by him at his will."

Do not think that I am proposing some form of Calvinism or even its watered-down cousin, Lordship Salvation. In no way do I intend to remove the working of the free will of man to choose to submit to God's truth and humble themselves to His glory. I am simply saying that repentance is the work of God that changes the heart, the part which man cannot do on his own. The reason that so many are unable to make the changes they seek is because they are seeking them in dependence upon their own will to do so, it's not that they haven't repented enough, it's that they have not truly cast off their own thinking, seeing the actions as right for some other reason than that God has said so. They have mixed their own reasoning with His word and exalted themselves alongside of God and their humility is false before Him. There most certainly are alternate reasons to want to stop sin, the consequences of it ruin the life, there is just no way to use God as your excuse if you are not fully sold out to His truth. If you are to experience genuine conversion by God then it must be with Him as God in truth and nothing less. When this is the case then temptations will fade away because your love for God has become pure and your view of the flesh has become real.

WHAT DOES LOVING GOD LOOK LIKE?

Do you love God? Of course, you say that you do or you wouldn't have read this far in a book such as this, but do you really? Let's use God's Word as a mirror for a minute and see what it says. How do you love God according to Him?

Exodus 20:6 "And shewing mercy unto thousands of them that love me, and keep my commandments."

John 14:15 "If ye love me, keep my commandments."

John 14:21 "He that hath my commandments, and keepeth them, he it is that loveth me: and he that loveth me shall be loved of my Father, and I will love him, and will manifest myself to him.

John 15:9-10 "As the Father hath loved me, so have I loved you: continue ye in my love. If ye keep my commandments, ye shall abide in my love; even as I have kept my Father's commandments, and abide in his love."

1 John 2:3-6 "And hereby we do know that we know him, if we keep his commandments. He that saith, I know him, and keepeth not his commandments, is a liar, and the truth is not in him. But whoso keepeth his word, in him verily is the love of God perfected: hereby know we that we are in him. He that saith he abideth in him ought himself also so to walk, even as he walked."

There can be no question that loving God means that you will keep His commandments, both the Old and the New Testaments teach this truth. Many make the error though that if a person does works it means they love, which is backward from what the Bible teaches. We see in the Bible, rather, that if you love God, you will be obedient to His command.

Obedience isn't always works; sometimes it is abstinence instead. However, to focus on the works is not only wrong, but it misses the point that God is presenting.

We understand from the teaching of Paul to the Romans that the law is a schoolmaster to bring us to repentance, but that isn't the end of the story. The law does not cease to be useful once we have come to repentance. At that point, it becomes more glorious, not in the keeping of it to attain salvation, but in the usefulness of it in the instruction of love. If I love God, I will not put anything else before Him. I will not worship anything but Him, nor will I ever blaspheme Him. Do you get the picture? The commandment not only points out my sinfulness, it also is a guide to show me how to love God. The same is true with mankind: if I love you, I will not dishonor you, I will not kill you, I will not steal from you, I will not lie to you, I will not commit adultery with your wife, and on we could go. The commandments teach us how to love God and how to love others. What then of those who despise the commandments of God, those who say that since we are under grace, we no longer need God's commandments? That is just as foolish as buying a building kit and throwing away the instructions: you may build something, but chances are it will not be what it could have been and it may not even work at all. Those extra pieces were not supposed to be extra, you know.

Do you remember how we defined iniquity? Iniquity is a negative attitude toward righteousness and a positive attitude toward wickedness. The Ten Commandments work as a sliding scale to reveal the sincerity of our love or our iniquity, if you will allow me some latitude in illustration.

Let me explain this by looking at the Ten Commandments for a minute. Consider the commandments here along with a summery thought on each.

Thou shalt not have any other Gods before me – Love Me – Inward attitude

Thou shalt not make any graven image – Worship Me

Thou shalt not take the name of the Lord thy God in vain – Praise Me rather than curse Me.

Remember the Sabbath to keep it holy – Keep My holiness

Honor your father and your mother – Obey those in authority, your parents are your first authority.

Thou shalt not kill – Don't kill

Thou shalt not commit adultery – Don't betray

Thou shalt not steal – Don't steal

Thou shalt not bear false witness – Don't lie

Thou shalt not covet – Don't lust – Inward attitude

Do you notice here how the commandments are end-capped with attitudes and that these attitudes are fulfilled with actions? You can work your way from either end, both positive and negatively. If you love God you will worship him, you will praise him, you will keep His Holiness, you will obey those in authority, you will... put away lust.

You can work your way backward in a negative fashion though, as well. If you give into your lusts you will lie, you will steal, you will betray, you will kill, you will disobey those in authority you will... not love God. Do you see how this issue of loving God is diametrically opposed to yielding to your lusts? You either love God and seek to please Him or you love self and seek to fulfill your lusts. Jesus put it so succinctly when He taught.

Matthew 6:19-24 "Lay not up for yourselves treasures upon earth, where moth and rust doth corrupt, and where thieves break through and steal: But lay up for yourselves treasures in heaven, where neither moth nor rust doth corrupt, and where thieves do not break through nor steal: For where your treasure is, there will your heart be also. The light of the body is the eye: if therefore thine eye be single, thy whole body shall be full of light. But if thine eye be evil, thy whole body shall be full of darkness. If therefore the light that is in thee be darkness, how great is that darkness! No man can serve two masters: for either he will hate the one, and love the other; or else he will hold to the one, and despise the other. Ye cannot serve God and mammon."

The question that every person must answer is, what is the light of your eye, who is your master? If you love God with all your heart, soul and mind, that leaves nothing to love self, and as such, there is then no temptation that can overcome you. In that way, you will keep God's commandments as a guide to loving Him. Anyone who sees the commandments of God as burdensome has missed what John the beloved saw: that true love removes the grief from the commandments because it has removed the love of self and is truly set on pleasing only God. There can be no doubt of this truth. Paul told Timothy that this was the ultimate purpose of the commandment, as well, and how understanding this would change one's understanding of the law completely.

1 Timothy 1:5-7 "Now the end of the commandment is charity out of a pure heart, and of a good conscience, and of faith unfeigned: From which some having swerved have turned aside unto vain jangling; Desiring to be teachers of the law; understanding neither what they say, nor whereof they affirm."

So many misunderstand the law and either ignore it altogether or make it the source of righteousness. The law can never provide righteousness, which comes by imputation from Christ alone, but it does provide us a guide whereby we may know how to love God in the fullest fashion, and thus, keep the law to its purpose. In doing so, we shall not only be pleasing to God, but we will also receive reward of Him.

James 1:12 "Blessed is the man that endureth temptation: for when he is tried, he shall receive the crown of life, which the Lord hath promised to them that love him."

James 1:2-4 "My brethren, count it all joy when ye fall into divers temptations; Knowing this, that the trying of your faith worketh patience. But let patience have her perfect work, that ye may be perfect and entire, wanting nothing."

THE GREAT WARNINGS

The result of abandoning this double-minded approach is that we are able to finally draw near to God in genuine faith, and when we do, He lifts us up. He gives us the stability that we could not find by the pursuit of our lusts. There are four warnings given following this promise. First, don't try to see if others are doing this before you go forward. Too often we look at others and start judging what we see in them instead of correcting our own problems. If you are worried about what others are doing, you will not get the help that you need. Instead you will stagnate in your justification of your sins and you will eventually repeat the cycle. This warning is found in James 4:11-12.

"Speak not evil one of another, brethren. He that speaketh evil of his brother, and judgeth his brother, speaketh evil of the law, and judgeth the law: but if thou judge the law, thou art not a doer of the law, but a judge. There is one lawgiver, who is able to save and to destroy: who art thou that judgest another?"

So many people get caught up in the comparison cycle, judging ourselves among ourselves. Paul warns of that in 2 Corinthians 10:12, "For we dare not make ourselves of the number, or compare ourselves with some that commend themselves: but they measuring themselves by themselves, and comparing themselves among themselves, are not wise." We must remember that Christ alone is the standard by which we are to measure. It is His image that we are to be conformed to and not that of those we attend church with. If we compare ourselves to a false standard, we will be lifted up in our own estimation rather than keeping our heart humble before God.

The second warning is found in verses 13-16, which says,

53

"Go to now, ye that say, To day or to morrow we will go into such a city, and continue there a year, and buy and sell, and get gain: Whereas ye know not what shall be on the morrow. For what is your life? It is even a vapour, that appeareth for a little time, and then vanisheth away. For that ye ought to say, If the Lord will, we shall live, and do this, or that. But now ye rejoice in your boastings: all such rejoicing is evil."

This warning is that you had better not put off getting things right in your life. You don't know how long you have to do right. We often think that we have a long time to get things right or make changes in our life, but we simply might not. Life itself is uncertain, and you might not even have the rest of today. We have all known people who intended to do good things only to never accomplish them because they waited too long. You can waste your opportunity to have peace in this life if you take it for granted that you have more time.

The third warning is not to refuse to get right with God. It says in verse 17, "Therefore to him that knoweth to do good, and doeth it not, to him it is sin." The sad reality is that some will simply refuse to do what they now know they should. They will instead justify or simply refuse to make any change. What they are saying is that they don't believe the Bible, they don't trust God, and they will not forsake their evil ways. This, of course, is willful sin, and it bears note to share what Hebrews 12:26-27 says about this.

"For if we sin wilfully after that we have received the knowledge of the truth, there remaineth no more sacrifice for sins, But a certain fearful looking for of judgment and fiery indignation, which shall devour the adversaries."

The final warning that we see is in the first part of chapter five. If you don't see this passage for the warning that it is, then it seems very out of place in the midst of the discussion. The first six verses could be summarized in this thought: that we should avoid trusting in worldly things to deal with our trials. This is not presented in the same fashion as the other warnings because if the Bible were to state it in the same fashion, then you would question it to a greater degree than you already do. Instead of warning the poor that they won't be satisfied with riches, God turns the conversation around and brings to light the conflict of the rich.

James 5:1-6 "Go to now, ye rich men, weep and howl for your miseries that shall come upon you. Your riches are corrupted, and your garments are motheaten. Your gold and silver is cankered; and the rust of them shall be a witness against you, and shall eat your flesh as it were fire. Ye have heaped treasure together for the last days. Behold, the hire of the labourers who have reaped down your fields, which is of you kept back by fraud, crieth: and the cries of them which have reaped are entered into the ears of the Lord of sabaoth. Ye have lived in pleasure on the earth, and been wanton; ye have nourished your hearts, as in a day of slaughter. Ye have condemned and killed the just; and he doth not resist you."

There are lessons for us to learn here, which, if not accepted as truth, will leave us open to be deceived by the allure of riches. We notice in the first verse of this passage that riches cannot prevent miseries. The rich experience sorrow just as anyone does, and trusting in riches creates a false hope that troubles can be avoided. The rich think they can buy out of troubles and the poor think that if they had riches they could, as well; neither are correct. The truth is that riches are a false covering. Just as John says in Revelation 3:17, "Because thou sayest, I am rich, and increased with goods, and have need of nothing; and knowest not that thou art wretched, and miserable, and poor, and blind, and naked:" Worldly goods are a poor substitute for security. On any given day, billions of dollars could evaporate from the stock market, the housing market could crash, as well as any other measure of wealth.

You cannot trust in money, power or position to save you from trials. No, we must reject the natural inclination to trust in our own devises and instead put our trust in the LORD. It says in Psalm 20:7, "Some trust in chariots, and some in horses: but we will remember the name of the LORD our God." Remember, God is the only source of confidence that does not change, and riches will never prevent the judgment that we will receive when we stand before Him. We will all stand before God, both lost and saved. The lost will be judged for their sins and condemned to everlasting punishment, and the saved will be judged according to what they have done with their opportunity to serve Him.

You see, just as James says, God knows our practices, He knows how we treat the poor, and He knows how we conduct our business. He knows whether we are living it up in the pleasures of this world, and He knows if we are given to fulfilling our lustful immorality and growing our hearts in worldliness. You certainly cannot hide the condition of your heart from God no matter how much your gold rings in the offering plates. The truth is that the more you indulge yourself in the pleasures of this world, the more you will be turned away from the people of God, as well. You may be in the fellowship of a church today, but if you pursue the riches of this world, then eventually you will condemn those who seek after righteousness.

You see excuses and temptation come in every variety. It is not just the lust for immoral behavior that we are tempted to, but rather the essence of temptation is simply to remove our heart from trusting wholly in God. Once we have done that, we are susceptible to any indulgence of the flesh. Once we have fallen from our faith in God, we will compare ourselves to others, we will neglect obedience, we will do that which we know is not right, and we will pursue the fulfillment of the flesh, even though we see the destructive fruit of it in every corner of our world. The person whose heart is set on God is pursuing true riches which the corruption of this world cannot take away.

DEALING WITH TRIALS

The discussion for the rest of chapter 5 turns to the issue of patience. This brings us back to another place that we started in chapter 1 verses 3-4.

"Knowing this, that the trying of your faith worketh patience. But let patience have her perfect work, that ye may be perfect and entire, wanting nothing."

One thing that is done in ships to minimize the effect that the waves have on the boat is to build them with a deeper keel. A keel is the structure along the centerline at the bottom of a vessel's hull, upon which the rest of the hull is built, extended downward as a blade or ridge to increase stability for the ship. In other words, the deeper the keel, the more stability the boat will have and the less the waves will toss it when they get into rough seas.

This is much like patience in our lives. When faith is properly placed in God rather than in the changing things of this world, then it is like building a deep keel on our boat of life. When the storm rages around us, we are not moved as much because we have developed a deeper trust in God that stabilizes us against the trials. The only way to develop patience is to have our faith tried, but if our faith is genuine, and we see that the trials do not upset our boat, we will develop a greater patience in the storms because of seeing the effectiveness of our faith. When we face a greater storm the next time, we are less affected because of the proving of our faith that produced patience in us. This truth is shown to us in Romans 5:3-5

"And not only so, but we glory in tribulations also: knowing that tribulation worketh patience; And patience, experience; and experience, hope: And hope maketh not ashamed;

because the love of God is shed abroad in our hearts by the Holy Ghost which is given unto us."

There are three examples of patience given to us in chapter five. The first is short, but it is something that most people can relate to: agriculture. It says in verse 7, "Be patient therefore, brethren, unto the coming of the Lord. Behold, the husbandman waiteth for the precious fruit of the earth, and hath long patience for it, until he receive the early and latter rain." If you have ever planted a seed, then you know that it takes time for the fruit to come. You plant, you water, you fertilize, you pull the weeds around it, and eventually it begins to put on blossoms, which are pollinated, and the fruit starts to grow. Finally, after a long process you are able to enjoy what you have looked forward to. This is how enduring the trials of life is supposed to work. You have sowed your seed of faith in God, and as the storms rise you let the roots grow deeper, you are to continue going through the process of growing until eventually you see fruit.

An impatient gardener loses interest. They stop tending the garden and weeds overtake it. They stop watering the plants, which wither and die. They never harvest the fruit they could have because they did not continue to do what they were supposed to do. Patience that is produced by seeing our faith endure trials causes us to be good gardeners in life, tending to those things that are important and not letting them die or become overgrown by weeds.

The second and third examples given are of the prophets. It says in verse 10 "Take, my brethren, the prophets, who have spoken in the name of the Lord, for an example of suffering affliction, and of patience. Behold, we count them happy which endure." These are examples of two men who did right despite affliction, and as a result, they were rewarded in their lives. They both suffered trials in different ways but they both found that God was the right place to put their trust instead of in the shaky things of this world.

The first prophet addressed is Job, in verses 11-16

"Ye have heard of the patience of Job, and have seen the end of the Lord; that the Lord is very pitiful, and of tender mercy. But above all things, my brethren, swear not, neither by heaven, neither by the earth, neither by any other oath: but let your yea be yea; and your nay, nay; lest ye fall into condemnation. Is any among you afflicted? let him pray. Is any merry? let him sing psalms. Is any sick among you? let him call for the elders of the church; and let them pray over him, anointing him with oil in the name of the Lord: And the prayer of faith shall save the sick, and the Lord shall raise him up; and if he have committed sins, they shall be forgiven him. Confess your faults one to another, and pray one for another, that ye may be healed. The effectual fervent prayer of a righteous man availeth much."

We learn a few things from what James tells us about Job concerning how to have patience in a trial. According to what James reveals here, we should always first consider the end of the trial rather than the present situation. It says, "Ye have heard of the patience of Job, and have seen the end of the Lord; that the Lord is very pitiful, and of tender mercy." Remember that God wants to bless you, not destroy you. Trials are not forever; there is an end to them all and for the faithful God will show mercy.

We are then told not to make promises but rather to simply speak the truth. So many people make promises in times of trial, that if God will just get them out of their problems, they will do this or that. God doesn't want you to try and bargain with Him; He wants you to deepen your faith and develop patience which will bring stability and maturity to your life.

61

The third thing we see in this passage about how Job dealt with his trial is that he was a man of prayer. Prayer is a great indicator of where our faith is: do we complain about it to others or do we make supplication to God? Who are we really trusting in? So often our hope is in men rather than in God because that is who we talk to about our problems. These verses do indicate that there is a time to ask others to pray for us, but we should be very careful about asking for them to solve our problem rather than allowing God to finish the work that He is doing in trying our faith.

Finally, concerning Job, we see that there is a need for self-examination during our trials. It tells us here to confess our faults one to another. Your faults are your sinful weaknesses, those areas that you have not been trusting God in. The purpose here is not to make yourself vulnerable to others, but rather that acknowledging of the areas in which you are weak will help you to strengthen yourself in those places. The goal is that asking others to help you and hold you accountable, while praying for you so that you can remove any hypocritical error that you have, will help you to develop genuine faith in that area.

The second example of a prophet that is given here is that of Elias, or as we might know him from the Old Testament, Elijah. It says in verses 17-20,

"Elias was a man subject to like passions as we are, and he prayed earnestly that it might not rain: and it rained not on the earth by the space of three years and six months. And he prayed again, and the heaven gave rain, and the earth brought forth her fruit. Brethren, if any of you do err from the truth, and one convert him; Let him know, that he which converteth the sinner from the error of his way shall save a soul from death, and shall hide a multitude of sins."

You might remember that Elijah was a man of extremes. The example here is that he prayed for it not to rain and it didn't rain for three years and six months. This was a significant issue for Israel because there were no rivers that could be counted on to bring water for the crops. They were heavily dependent upon rain to cause things to grow and provide pasture for the animals. Finally, when there was an acknowledgement of God's power, Elijah prayed again and God sent the rain. During this time, the Bible tells us that even though the land was in drought, God provided for Elijah in miraculous ways. First, by having ravens bring Him food, and then by making a widow's food last so that they both ate continually when it should have run out.

One truth to notice here is that in times of trials, God wants to do miraculous things in our lives. He wants us to see His provision when the world says that it is impossible. But that will not happen unless we have our eyes on Him instead of on the things of this world. It will not happen unless we have our confidence in Him instead of in things that fail. Once again, we see here, just like in the life of Job, that there is great power in prayer as it reveals the source of our confidence. Remember, our tongue brings up what is in our heart, either revealing envy and strife or revealing prayers of faith. One of the greatest evidences that our faith is sure is how this book ends by reminding us that we are to be witnesses of these truths to others, and that when we show our faith as true, it will cause others to be converted and cover a multitude of sins.

This illustration of facing the storms of life is used many times in the Bible. Before we end, I want you to consider one more passage that I believe gives such a powerful message of hope concerning having faith in God during the storms of life. It says in Psalm 107:23-31,

"They that go down to the sea in ships, that do business in great waters; These see the works of the LORD, and his wonders in the deep. For he commandeth, and raiseth the stormy wind, which lifteth up the waves thereof. They mount up to the heaven, they go down again to the depths: their soul is melted because of trouble. They reel to and fro, and stagger like a drunken man, and are at their wits' end. Then they cry unto the LORD in their trouble, and he bringeth them out of their distresses. He maketh the storm a calm, so that the waves thereof are still. Then are they glad because they be quiet; so he bringeth them unto their desired haven. Oh that men would praise the LORD for his goodness, and for his wonderful works to the children of men!"

You have two options when you face the temptations and trials of life: you can let them toss you up and down so that your soul melts because of your trouble until you are at your wits end, or you can cry to the LORD and allow Him to bring you out of your distresses to your desired haven. You don't have to be subject to the storms if you will remove the iniquity of your heart and have a genuine faith in God.

HOW TO DEAL WITH STRESS

Psalm 4:1-8 To the chief Musician on Neginoth, A Psalm of David. "Hear me when I call, O God of my righteousness: thou hast enlarged me when I was in distress; have mercy upon me, and hear my prayer. O ye sons of men, how long will ye turn my glory into shame? how long will ye love vanity, and seek after leasing? Selah. But know that the LORD hath set apart him that is godly for himself: the LORD will hear when I call unto him. Stand in awe, and sin not: commune with your own heart upon your bed, and be still. Selah. Offer the sacrifices of righteousness, and put your trust in the LORD. There be many that say, Who will shew us any good? LORD, lift thou up the light of thy countenance upon us. Thou hast put gladness in my heart, more than in the time that their corn and their wine increased. I will both lay me down in peace, and sleep: for thou, LORD, only makest me dwell in safety."

The number one contributor to health issues in the United States is stress. Some doctors say that up to 80% of health issues are stress related. The word stress itself is not in the King James Bible, but that doesn't mean that the Scriptures don't address the topic. In our text, we see the word distress, and of course it isn't hard to see that the root word here is, in fact, stress.

According to the Oxford Dictionary this word means, "[1]The action or fact of straining or pressing tightly, strain, stress, pressure; fig. pressure employed to produce action, constraint, compulsion;" The last part of this definition intrigued me: "pressure employed to produce action". Stress certainly does produce action in us, but generally not the type that it should. In our Psalm, David says that God had enlarged him when he was in distress, which is an interesting statement. The implication is that God wants to use stressors

65

in our lives to cause us to grow, or as the definition says, to put pressure on us to produce action. The problem is that we often allow it to produce the wrong actions.

Stress, it would seem, is like a magnifying lens: it can be focused on enlarging us but often we turn it toward our problems instead and magnify them. What then was intended by God to make us better is used to make our problems bigger. We see both of these examples given in the scriptures. In the reign of King Saul, the conflict with the Philistines was hard. The Prophet Samuel told Saul to take the army to a certain place and wait for him there. The Bible tells us that the people were under such a great stress in 1 Samuel 13:6 that "When the men of Israel saw that they were in a strait, (for the people were distressed,) then the people did hide themselves in caves, and in thickets, and in rocks, and in high places, and in pits." The stress of the situation was so great that the men of war hid anywhere they could find. Saul was also under a great deal of stress, which resulted in the terrible error of a sacrifice that was not lawful for him to make at the time. Because of Saul's response to the stress, God said he would remove him from being king and replace him with David.

Other examples of how stress magnifies our problems and causes us to make bad decisions are recorded in the Bible, but you have many examples from your own life, as well. It wouldn't take much to convince you that stress is bad and can cause us to make bad decisions. I want to focus on the alternate side of that. We see great examples of how to deal with stress properly in the lives of Jacob and David.

Do you remember when Jacob was under a great stress as he headed back to see Esau? In that time, instead of making his own plans, Jacob turned to God, and we find one of the most incredible interactions a man ever had with God as Jacob wrestled with God all night long. He later said of this place in Genesis 35:3, "And let us arise, and go up to Bethel; and I will make there an altar unto God, who answered me in the day of my distress, and was with me in the way which I went." It was this encounter that changed Jacob's life and caused him to turn to God and become a man of great faith.

Likewise, David faced many times of stress in his life, but one in particular is called out in the Bible in a unique way. Just before God would make David the king over Israel He allowed David's city to be attacked by an enemy. The families of all David's men were carried away by the enemy and when the men saw this they were greatly grieved, as you would imagine. They were so grieved that they talked about turning on David and killing him. This passage carries a great statement of encouragement in it, though, as it says in 1 Samuel 30:6, "And David was greatly distressed; for the people spake of stoning him, because the soul of all the people was grieved, every man for his sons and for his daughters: but David encouraged himself in the LORD his God."

I don't know if you noticed, but in both of these instances, the stress was alleviated when Jacob and David turned away from the circumstances and toward God. The stress of their situation was great; like Saul, they could have allowed it to magnify their problems until they did wrong, but instead, they both turned to the Lord, and God delivered them from their problem. Instead of magnifying the problems, the stress was used to enlarge them, and both Jacob and David went on to become great for God, and these times of stress were a significant proving time for them in that. For just a minute, consider all the verses that tell us that this is a right response to stress.

2 Samuel 22:7 "In my distress I called upon the LORD, and cried to my God: and he did hear my voice out of his temple, and my cry did enter into his ears.

Psalm 25:17 "The troubles of my heart are enlarged: O bring thou me out of my distresses."

Psalm 107:6 "Then they cried unto the LORD in their trouble, and he delivered them out of their distresses."

Psalm 107:13 "Then they cried unto the LORD in their trouble, and he saved them out of their distresses."

Psalm 107:19 "Then they cry unto the LORD in their trouble, and he saveth them out of their distresses."

Psalm 107:28 "Then they cry unto the LORD in their trouble, and he bringeth them out of their distresses."

Psalm 118:5 "I called upon the LORD in distress: the LORD answered me, and set me in a large place."

Psalm 120:1 "A Song of degrees. In my distress I cried unto the LORD, and he heard me."

I hope you get the point that the desire of God is that when you face stress in your life, you would turn to Him. He wants to enlarge you, but if you don't turn to Him, you will turn that magnifying glass on your problems and enlarge them to the place that you make bad decisions and hurt yourself. In our text passage, we see the process that God desires for us to use to deal with stress very clearly.

Notice that in David's distress he called upon God, clearly asking God to hear his prayer in verse one. We have firmly established that this is the right response. What, though, are we to do in prayer? I'm sure that you, like me, have prayed about something that was stressing you out and didn't seem to get much relief. I never experienced relief because I was still focused on the issue rather than on God until I saw this passage in this light. Notice the six things that God says we should focus on in our prayer during times of stress.

First, he says in verse four "stand in awe". The problem that we have is that we are too often in awe of our problems, and David is not referring to that. Instead, he is telling us to stand in awe of God. You have a choice: you can see God from the perspective of your problems or you can see your problems from the perspective of your God. The one that seems bigger is the one that you are focused on. During times of stress, if you will get your focus back on how great God is, then it will change your perspective about how big your problems are. "Stand in awe" means that you remember that God is bigger than any problem; He is greater than any trial and He is able to deliver you from any stress. As a child of God, the only reason we face stress alone is because we have forgotten God. He has never forgotten you, though. The first step is to get your view back where it ought to be, relying on God and His power.

> "If you look at the world, you'll be distressed; if you look within you'll be depressed; but if you look at Christ, you'll be at rest."
> -Corrie Ten Boom

The second thing David says to us is "sin not". This sounds simple enough, but that is certainly the temptation during times of stress. The first step of sin in stress is that you stop trusting in God and start trusting in your own thinking. I shudder to think of all the times that I have made a plan to get myself out of a stressful time and how badly I have messed it up. David reminds us that if we don't get our eyes on God, then we are likely to make a sinful decision. What a good reminder that the alternative to turning to God in our stress is sinful.

The next instruction that we have from David is to "commune with your own heart upon your bed". This is a poetic way of saying, "meditate on what God is trying to teach you". In times of stress, God wants to enlarge you, He wants to make you greater than you have been before so the stress that He has allowed in your life is for that purpose. In those times then we are to meditate on what God is doing and in prayer seek to apply His Word to learn not only how to respond in the moment but what lesson God wants us to take that will make us better. There is no doubt that David was stressed many times in his life, and that is when God gave him many of the Psalms as answers. The meditation of David on what God was doing changed his thoughts from problems to praises.

Isaiah 30:20-21 "And though the Lord give you the bread of adversity, and the water of affliction, yet shall not thy teachers be removed into a corner any more, but thine eyes shall see thy teachers: And thine ears shall hear a word behind thee, saying, This is the way, walk ye in it, when ye turn to the right hand, and when ye turn to the left."

When we meditate on what God is doing, He will show us the teachers that He has placed in our life. So often we run from the lessons, but God wants to use these things to speak to us instead. I praise God for those times that I have been willing to meditate on what God was doing in my life through my stresses and learned great lessons that changed me for the better. Now I know many of my teachers, when they come around, I recognize them and know that they are there to help me not to hurt me. I am better able to prepare myself for the lesson in that fashion and be teachable in those times.

The fourth instruction by David here is that we would "be still". So often in our stress we run from God and try to run from our problems. My mother used to tell me, "No matter where you go, there you are." What she meant was that you cannot run from your problems; they will follow you. Stop trying to run away from stress and start looking to God for answers instead.

Psalm 46:10 "Be still, and know that I am God: I will be exalted among the heathen, I will be exalted in the earth."

God wants us to stop running all the time and just be still so that we can see Him do what needs to be done. You have only caused more issues by your constant plotting and moving during times of stress, but faith in God will solve the problem. Stop doing it on your own and look to God, know that He is God and not you, then He will be exalted and work on your behalf.

The fifth step that we see here is that during these times we should "Offer the sacrifices of righteousness". What would those be? It simply means to do what we know is right during times of stress. The flesh will try to get us to sin, accuse God, run away or remove ourselves from closeness with God. David says, however, that we should simply do what we know is right. In times of stress, that is a great sacrifice because everything that is in us wants to do the opposite. Some might call it character or discipline but God calls it a sacrifice here. The flesh and its desires are what you are sacrificing, and instead, you are living to God.

Finally, we are told to "put your trust in the LORD". This is kind of a summary of all the instruction that we have been given. Simply put, we are not to take matters into our own hands. We are to let God do what He will and trust that He always does right. I don't have to figure it out and make it work; I have to trust God and allow Him to do what He desires. God will work all things out for our good and for His glory if we wait on Him. There is no doubt that through my life I have created countless problems because I trusted in myself rather than in God. I so wish that I could go back and change that, but of course I cannot, and neither can you. Focusing on how we have messed it up before is not helpful except in learning the lesson not to do it that way again.

David goes on to say that there are many people who will question this method of dealing with stress. He says, "There be many that say, Who will shew us any good?" God already knows that when you start to deal with stress in this way, the people around you will try to get you to question the wisdom of it. Likewise, the Devil, who is the Accuser of the brethren, will tell you that it will never work. However, take heart because the Word of God is true; if you will stay the course, God will enlarge you in a way that you have never known. He will do as David says and lift up the light of His countenance upon you. When He does, David says that you will experience two great blessings.

First in verse 7 it says, "Thou hast put gladness in my heart, more than in the time that their corn and their wine increased." God will make you glad! The contrast here is given to show us something wonderful. The most gladness that the world has is when they are prospered. When their corn and wine increased, they see that as being enlarged and blessed. Unfortunately, there are many believers who fall prey to the idea that physical possessions are the sign of blessings, but David says that there is a gladness that exceeds

72

that of physical possessions. God wants you to experience more than this world can offer. He wants you to be a partaker of the spiritual blessings that only His children can share. Have you ever really experienced the joy of the Lord being your strength like David did? I mean the joy that fills your soul and overcomes you with gladness so that you sit and weep because of the overwhelming love of God for you. This is that joy unspeakable and full of glory that we sing about. You will never get that from possessions, I promise you. This gladness comes only from closeness with God and that closeness comes only from waiting on Him in times of stress.

The second blessing that we are promised is in verse 8, "I will both lay me down in peace, and sleep: for thou, LORD, only makest me dwell in safety." How many times in stress have you lost your sleep? How often in those times have you wished for peace but found none? That is because you were trusting in yourself and your own plans. When you do things God's way, He gives you peace and rest because there is no safer place than in His care. The security that comes from resting in God is described in the New Testament by Paul in Philippians 4:6-7

"Be careful for nothing; but in every thing by prayer and supplication with thanksgiving let your requests be made known unto God. And the peace of God, which passeth all understanding, shall keep your hearts and minds through Christ Jesus."

You can have the peace that passes understanding in the midst of your stresses if you will do what David showed you. Stress can begin to enlarge you by God's grace or you can continue to enlarge your problems because of it; the choice is yours.